Easy to Intermediate Piano Solo

THE WORLD'S GREAT CLASSICAL MUSIC

The Classical Era

64 Selections from Piano Literature, Symphonies, Concertos & Operas

for Piano Solo

EDITED BY BLAKE NEELY AND RICHARD WALTERS

Front Cover: Raphael, *Poetry*

ISBN 978-0-634-04807-4

7777 W. BLUEMOUND RD. P.O. BOX 13819 MILWAUKEE, WI 53213

Visit Hal Leonard online at
www.halleonard.com

CONTENTS

Transcriptions

Sonata in B-flat Major

Johann Christian Bach
1735-1782
Op. 5, No. 1

Allegretto

5

Tempo di minuetto

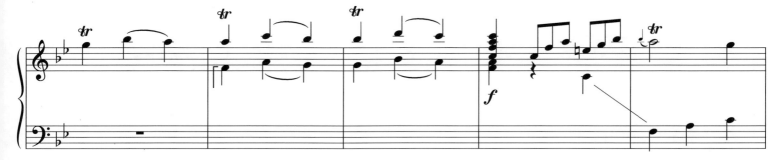

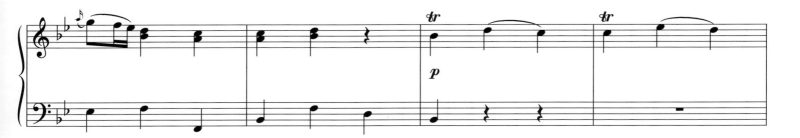

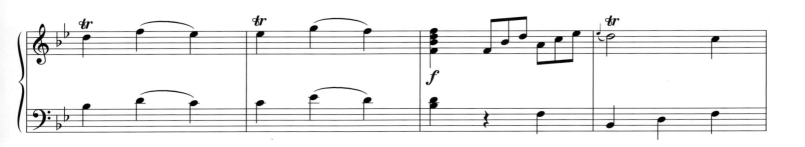

Bagatelle

Ludwig van Beethoven
1770–1827
Op. 119, No. 1

Allegretto

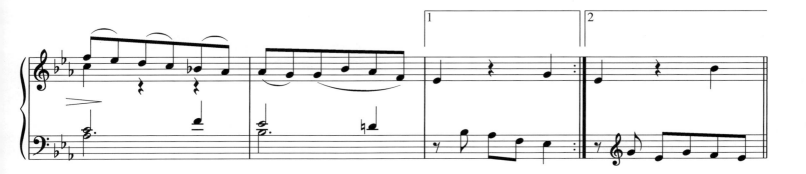

cresc.

Bagatelle

Ludwig van Beethoven
1770–1827
Op. 119, No. 4

Andante cantabile

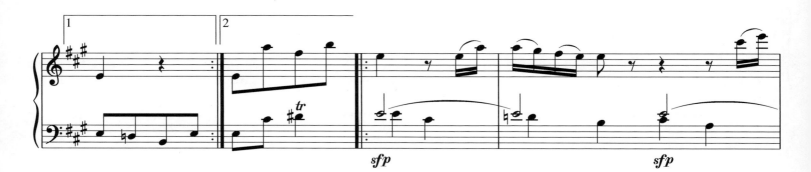

Country Dance No. 1

Ludwig van Beethoven
1770–1827

Bagatelle

Ludwig van Beethoven
1770–1827
Op. 33, No. 3

Allegretto

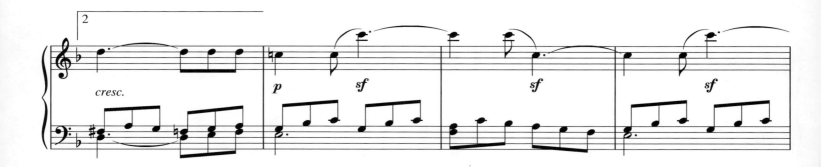

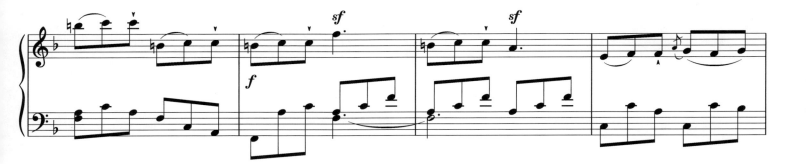

Ecossaise in E-flat Major

Ludwig van Beethoven
1770-1827
WoO 86

Allegretto

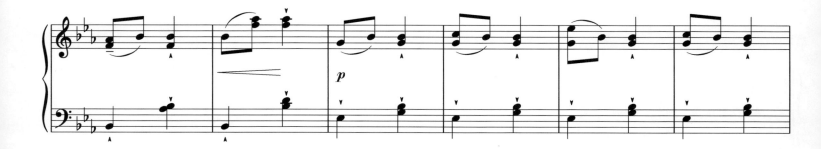

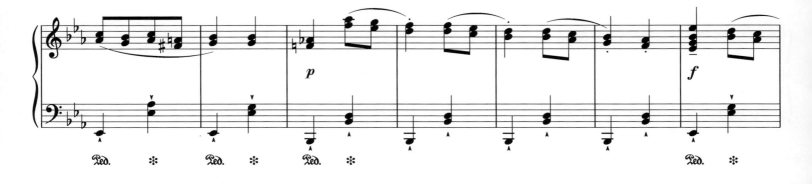

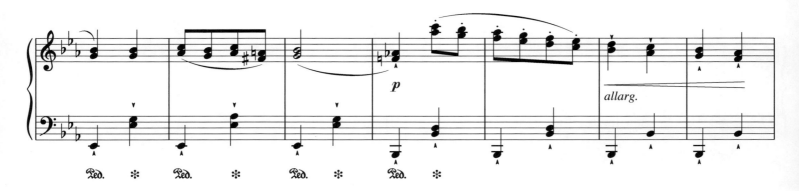

Tempo I

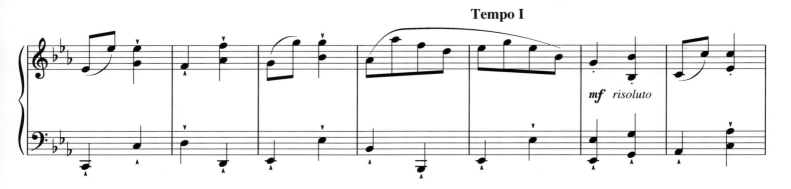

24

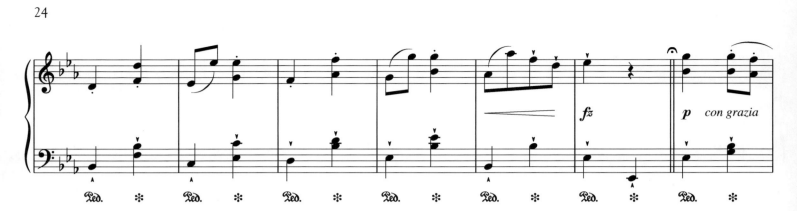

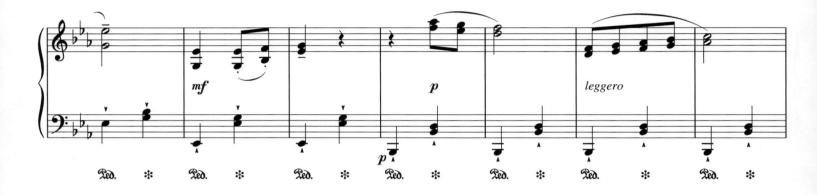

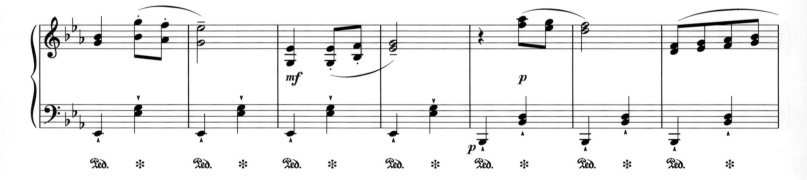

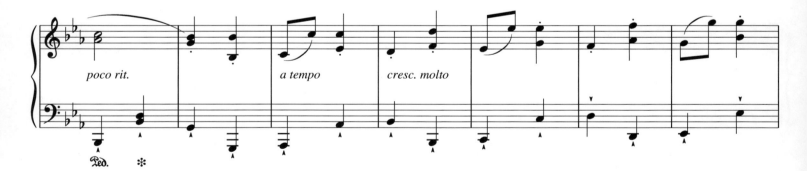

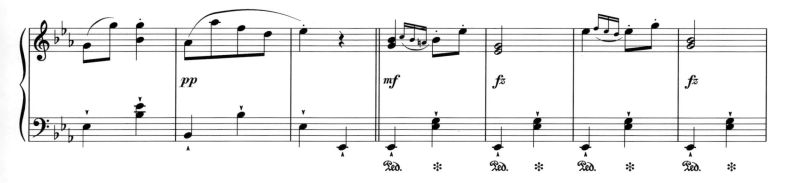

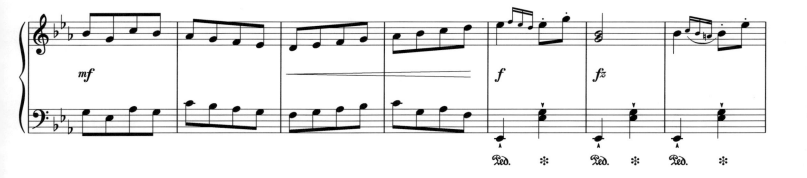

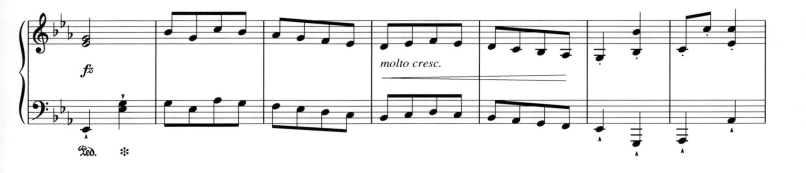

Ecossaise in G Major

Ludwig van Beethoven
1770-1827
WoO 23

Allegretto

Minuet in G Major

Ludwig van Beethoven
1770-1827

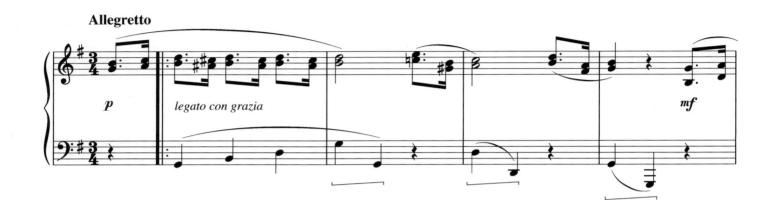

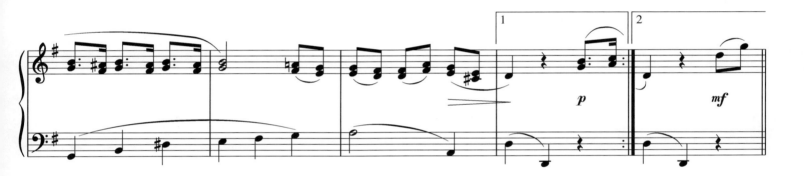

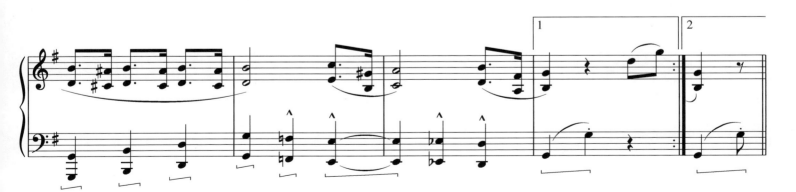

TRIO

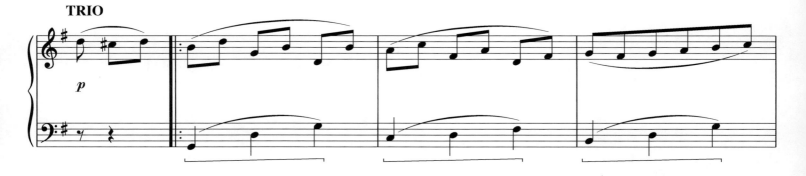

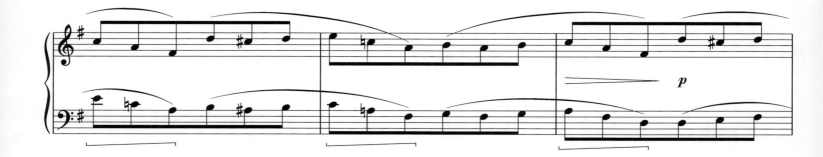

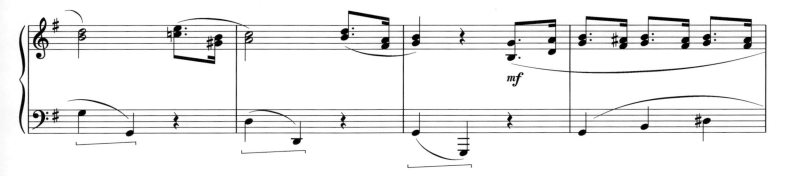

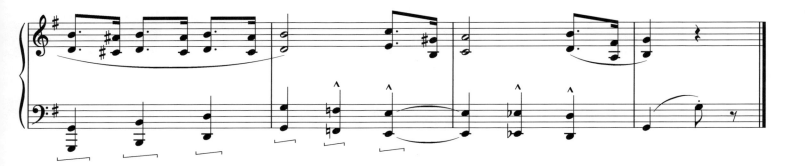

Für Elise
(For Elise)
Bagatelle in A minor

Ludwig van Beethoven
1770–1827
WoO 59

Poco moto

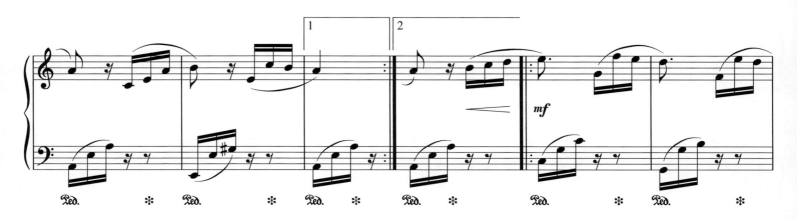

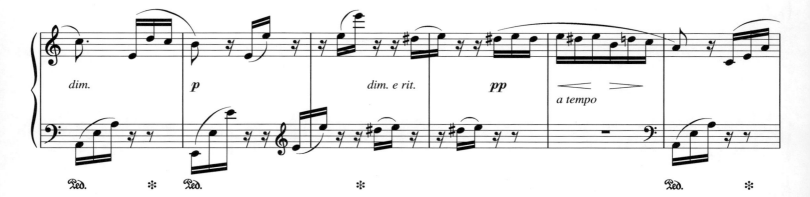

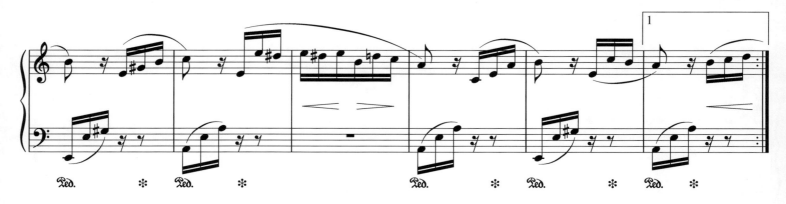

31

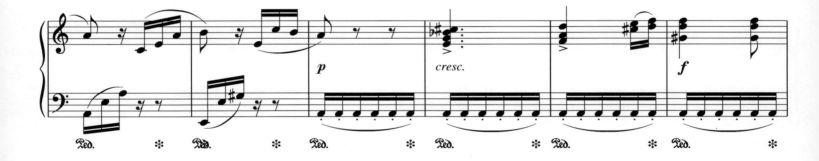

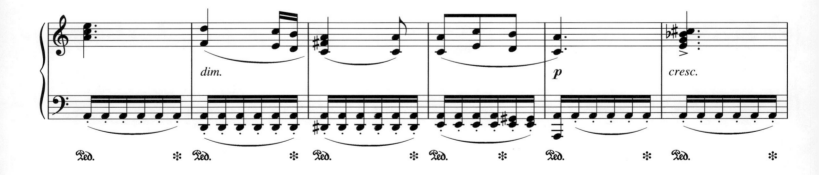

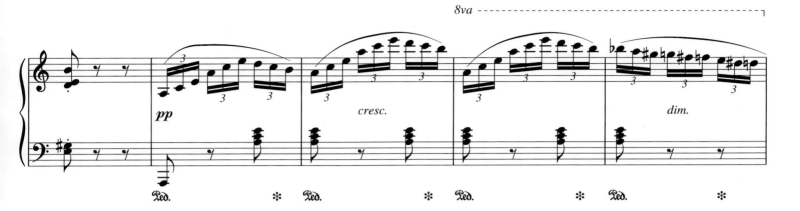

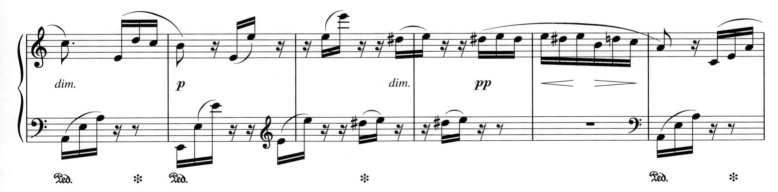

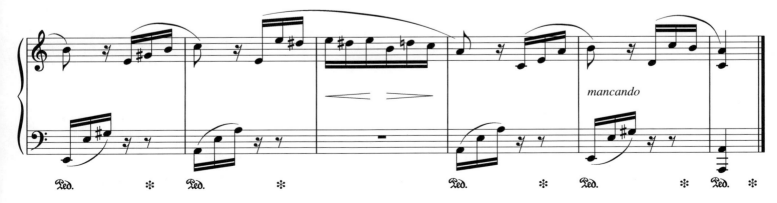

Sonata in G Minor

Ludwig van Beethoven
1770-1827
Op. 49, No. 1

Andante (♩ = 80-84)

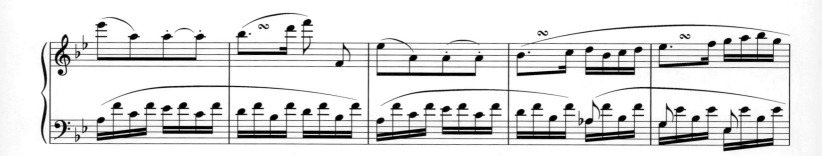

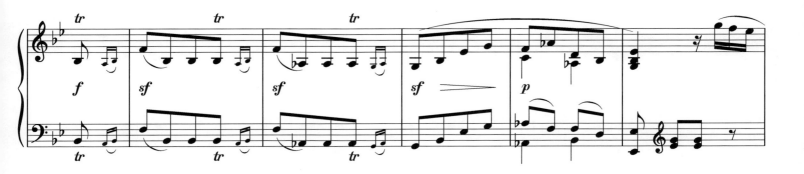

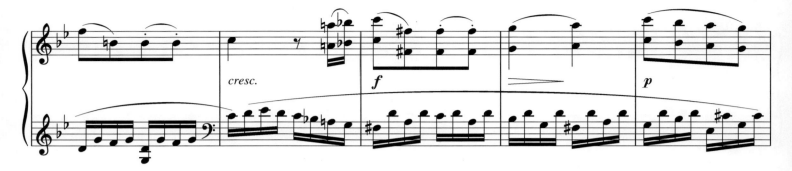

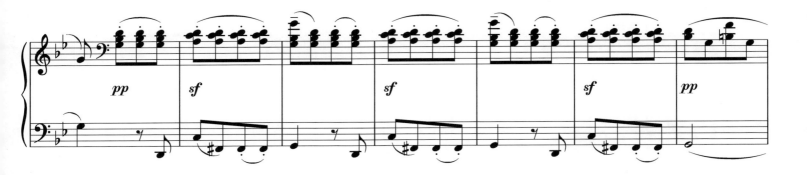

RONDO

Allegro ($\quad$. = 112)

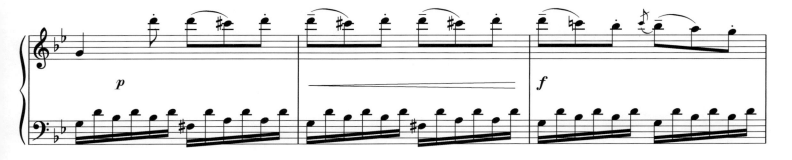

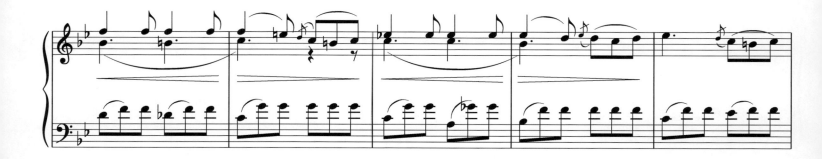

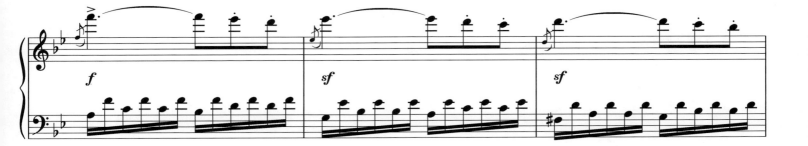

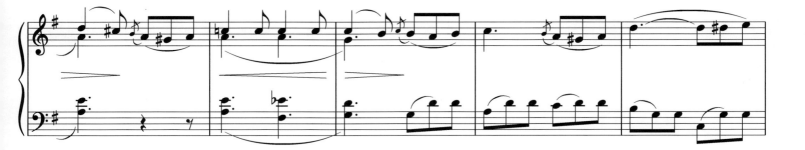

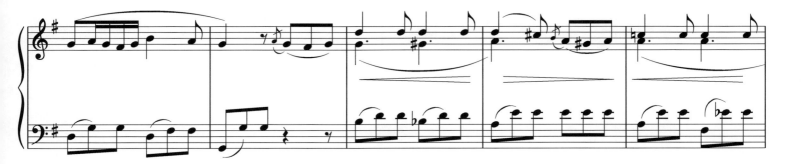

Sonatina in F Major

Ludwig van Beethoven
1770–1827

Allegro assai

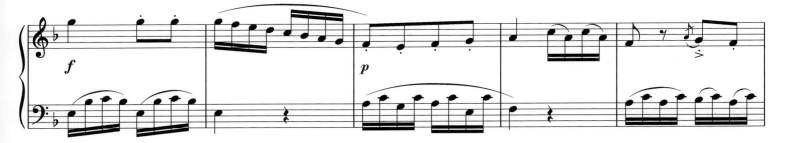

cresc.

Rondo

Allegro

p

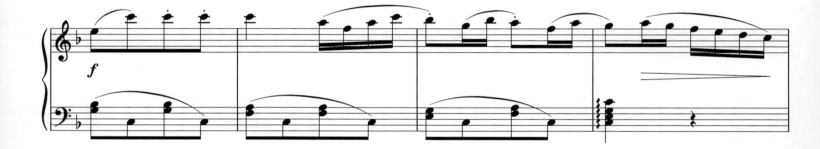

f

p

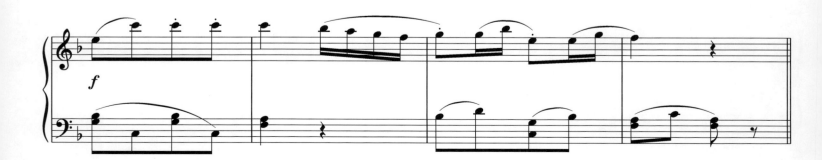

f

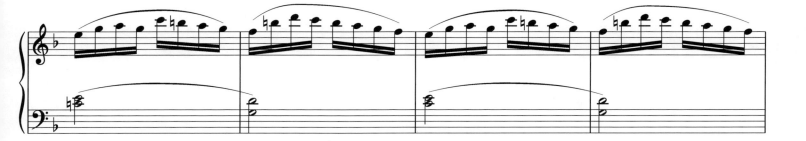

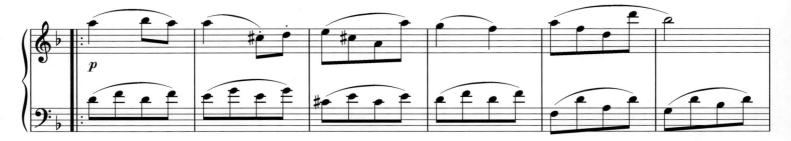

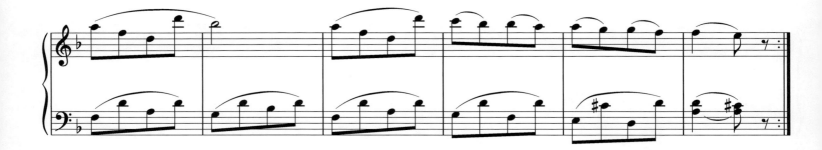

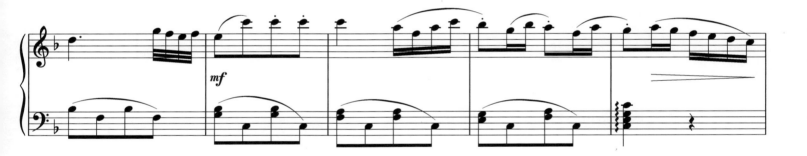

Sonata in G Major

Ludwig van Beethoven
1770-1827
Op. 49, No. 2

Allegro ma non troppo ($\bf \frac{1}{}$ = **84-88**)

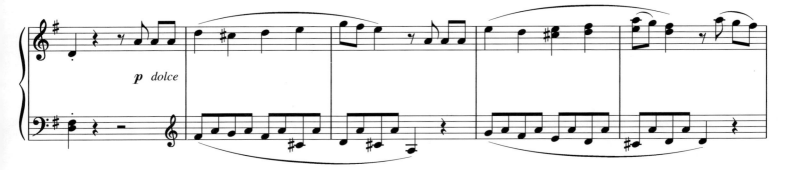

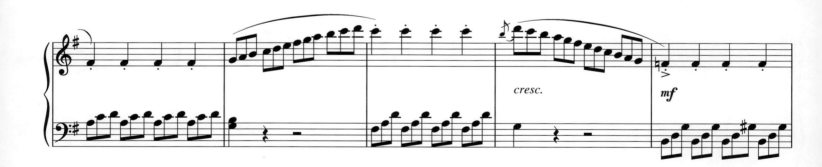

Tempo di Minuetto (♩ = 112-116)

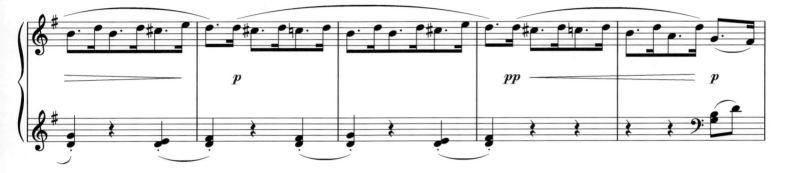

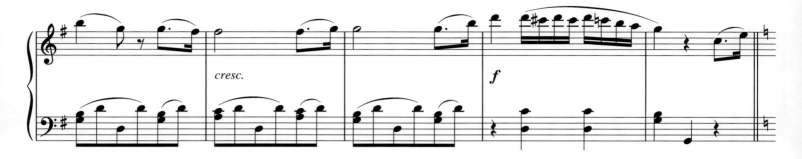

Sonatina in G Major

Ludwig van Beethoven
1770–1827

Moderato

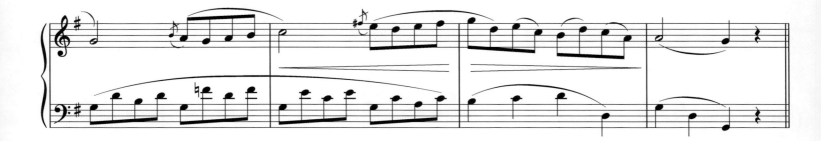

Romanza
Allegretto

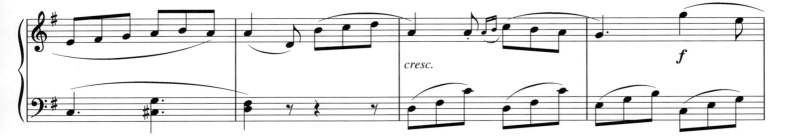

Variations on a Swiss Song

Ludwig van Beethoven
1770–1827
WoO 64

Theme

Andante con moto

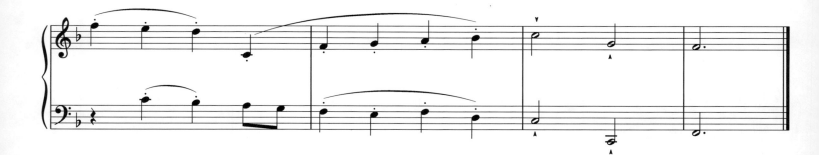

Var. I

Var. II

68

Var. III
Minore

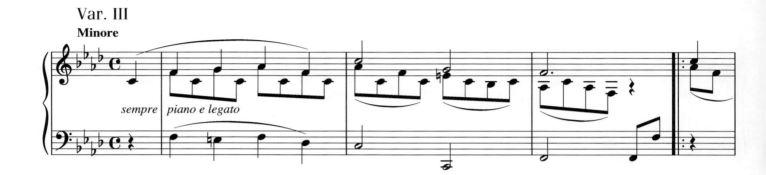

sempre piano e legato

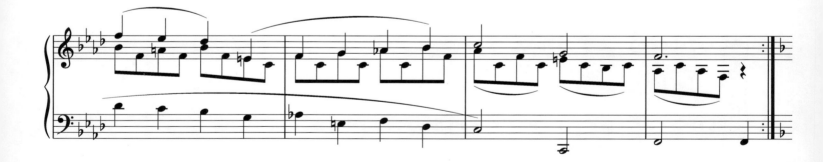

Var. IV
Maggiore

f

Var. V

sempre dolce

Var. VI

Arietta in C Major
from AN INTRODUCTION TO THE ART OF
PLAYING ON THE PIANOFORTE

Muzio Clementi
1752-1832
Op. 42

Allegretto

Monferrina in C Major

Muzio Clementi
1752–1832
WoO 15

Allegro con brio

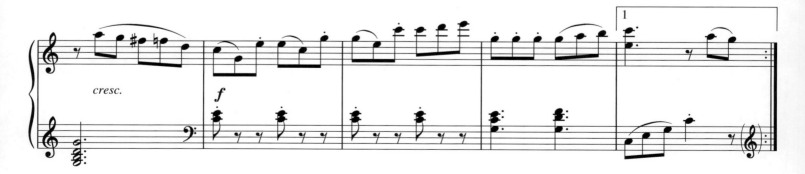

73

74

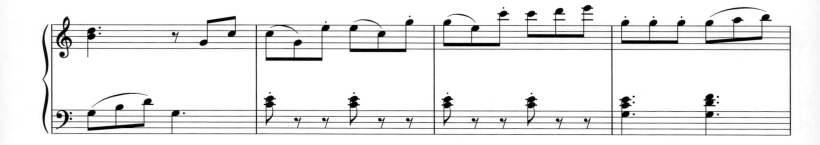

Spanish Dance
("Guaracha")
from AN INTRODUCTION TO THE ART OF
PLAYING ON THE PIANOFORTE

Muzio Clementi
1752-1832
Op. 42

Vivace

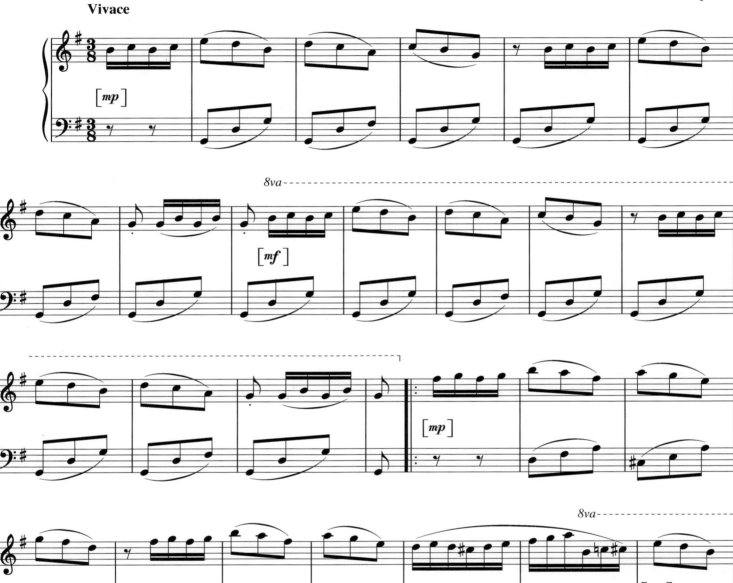

Sonatina in C Major

Muzio Clementi
1752-1832
Op. 36, No. 1

Spiritoso

77

Andante

Vivace

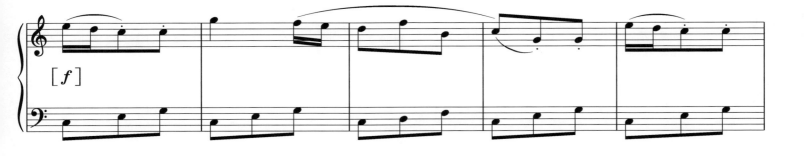

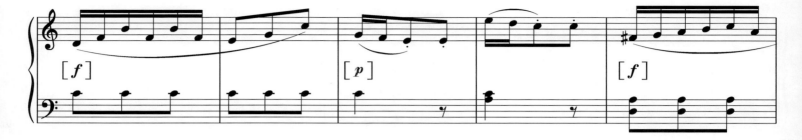

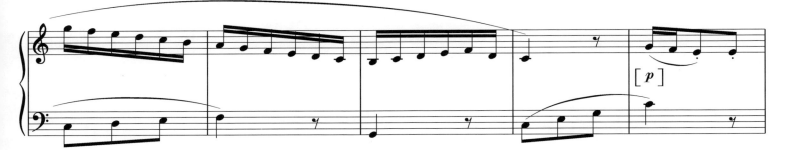

Sonatina in C Major

Muzio Clementi
1752-1832
Op. 36, No. 3

85

Un poco adagio

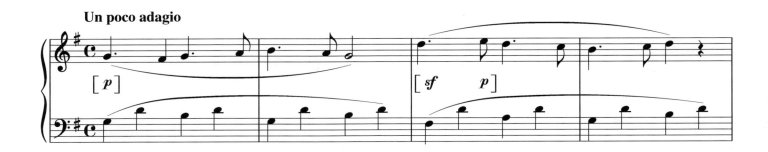

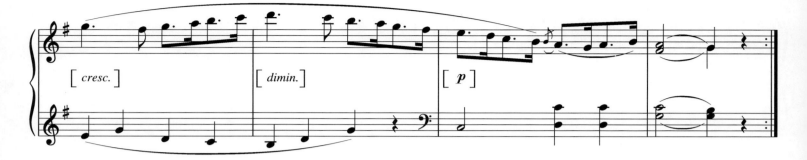

[*cresc.*]　　　　　[*dimin.*]　　　　　[***p***]

Allegro

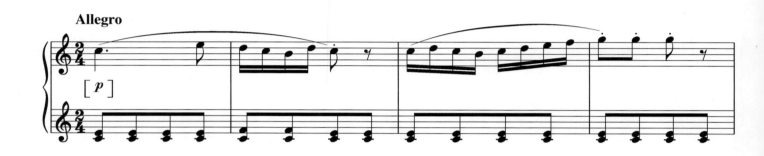

[***p***]

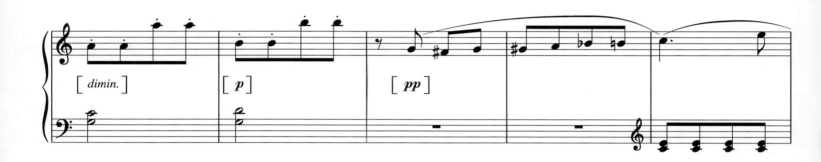

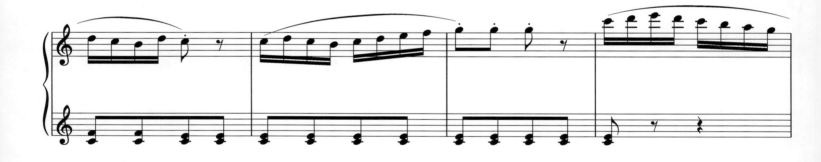

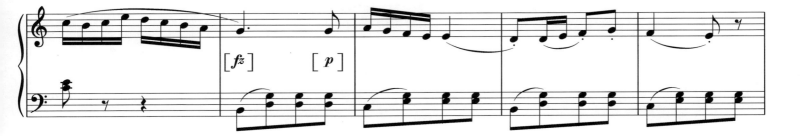

Sonata in G Major

Domenico Cimarosa
1749-1801

Sonatina in F Major

Anton Diabelli
1781–1858
Op. 168, No. 1

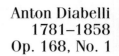

Moderato cantabile

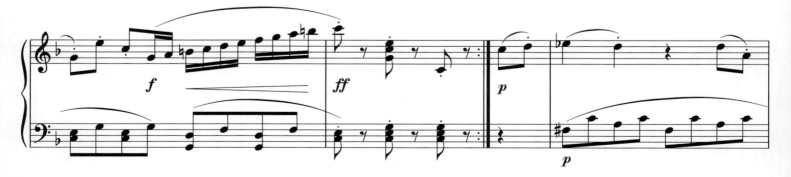

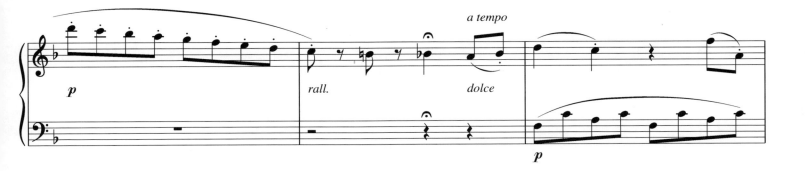

93

Andante cantabile

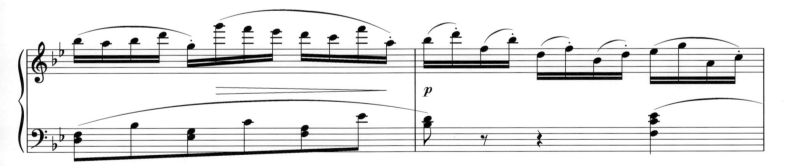

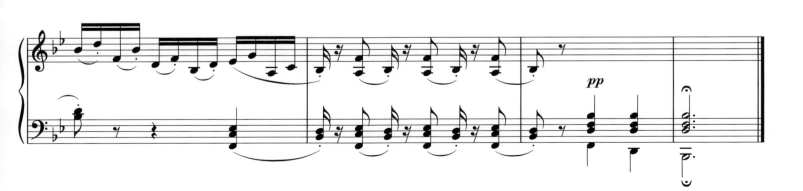

Rondo

Allegretto

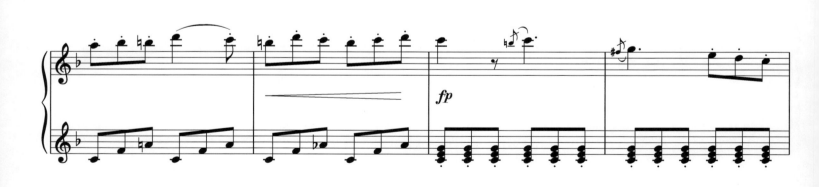

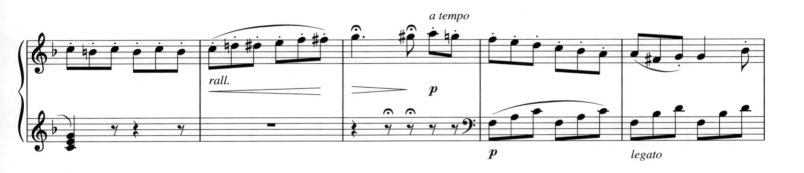

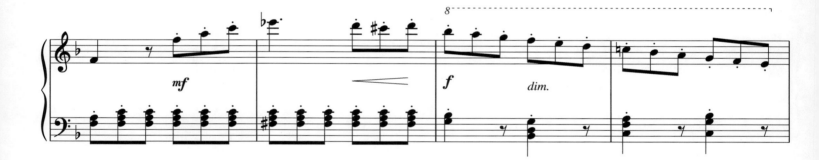

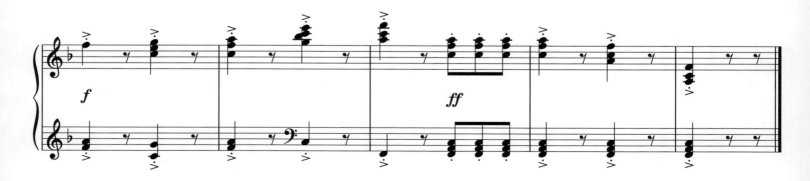

Spinning Song

(Spinnliedchen)

Albert Ellmenreich
1816–1905
Op. 14, No. 4

Allegretto

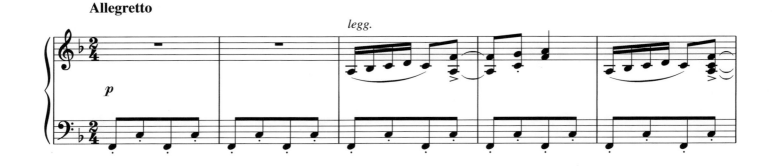

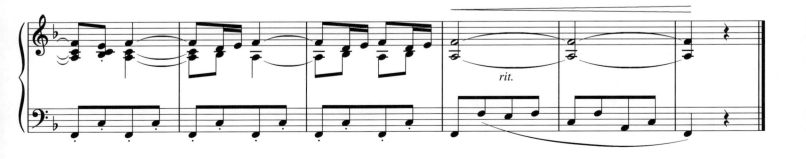

Country Dance

Franz Joseph Haydn
1732–1809

Allegretto

Sonata in C Major
First Movement

Franz Joseph Haydn
1732-1809
Hob. XVI/1

Allegro

sempre simile

cresc.

cresc.

Sonata in G Major

Franz Joseph Haydn
1732–1809
Hob. XVI/8

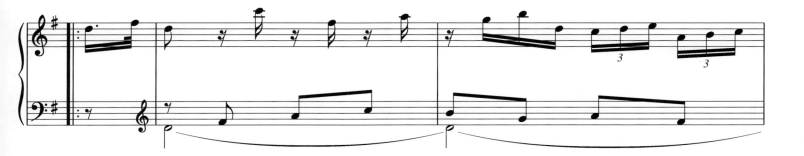

Minuet

[Tempo di minuetto]

[mp]

Allegro

[*mf*]

Air in A-flat Major
from LONDON NOTEBOOK

Wolfgang Amadeus Mozart
1756–1791
K. 109b, No. 8

[Andante]

[mp]

[mf]

[p]

Little Song

from NANNERL'S NOTEBOOK

Wolfgang Amadeus Mozart
1756–1791

[Andante con moto]

[p]

Allegro in B-flat Major

Wolfgang Amadeus Mozart
1756–1791
K. 3

[Allegro]

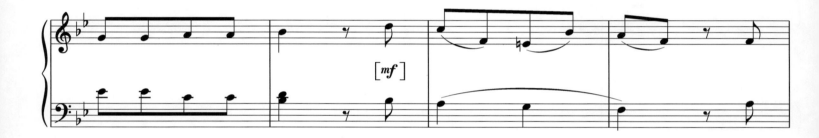

Funeral March for
Maestro Counterpoint

Wolfgang Amadeus Mozart
1756–1791
K. 453a

German Dance in C Major

Wolfgang Amadeus Mozart
1756–1791
K. 605, No. 3

[Allegro]

[f]

Fine

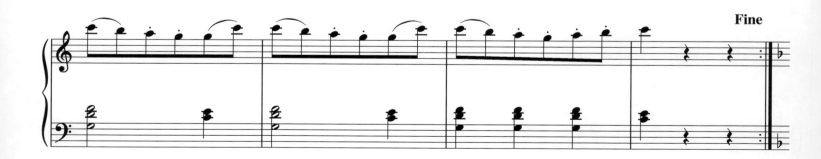

Trio (The Sleighride)

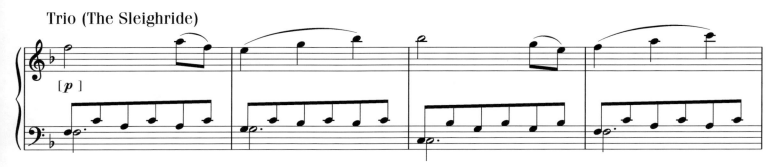

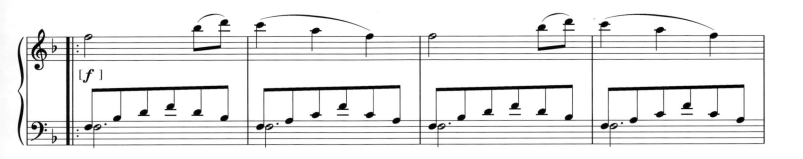

D.C. al Fine

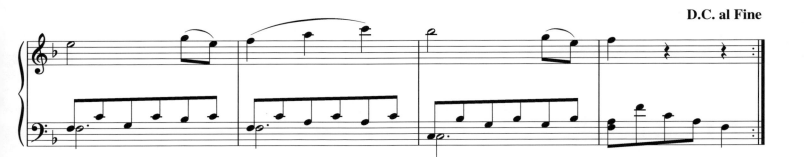

Minuet in C Major

Wolfgang Amadeus Mozart
1756–1791
K. 6

[Andante moderato]

Minuet in F Major

Wolfgang Amadeus Mozart
1756–1791
K. 2

[Allegretto]

Minuet in F Major

Wolfgang Amadeus Mozart
1756–1791

[Andante]

Minuet in G Major

Wolfgang Amadeus Mozart
1756–1791
K. 1

Presto in B-flat Major
from LONDON NOTEBOOK

Wolfgang Amadeus Mozart
1756–1791
K. 109b, No. 9

Presto

Rondo in C Major

Wolfgang Amadeus Mozart
1756–1791

[Allegro]

[mf]

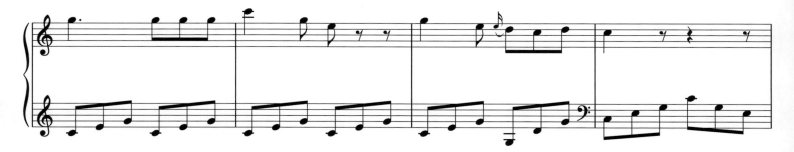

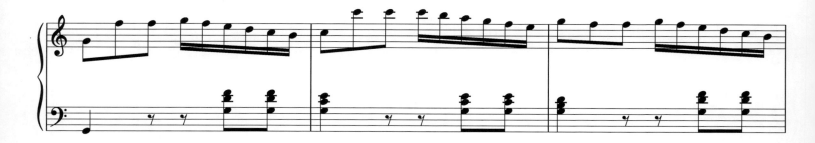

Waltz in A Major

Wolfgang Amadeus Mozart
1756–1791

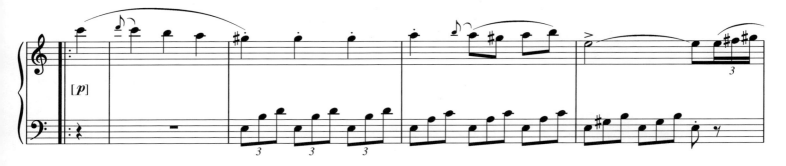

Waltz in D Major

Wolfgang Amadeus Mozart
1756–1791

Allegro moderato

Trio

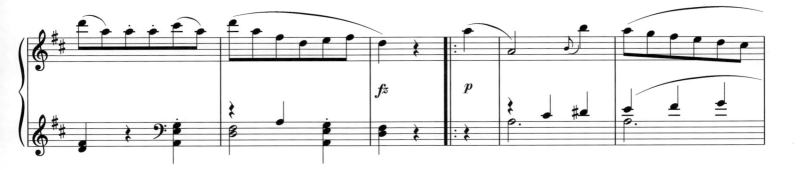

Children's Ballet

Daniel Gottlob Türk
1750–1813

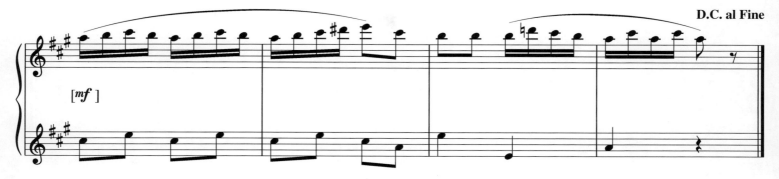

The Dancing Master

Daniel Gottlob Türk
1750–1813

Allegro moderato

Little Rondo

Daniel Gottlob Türk
1750-1813

Symphony No. 7

Second Movement Excerpt

Ludwig van Beethoven
1770-1827
Op. 92
originally for orchestra

Allegretto

cresc. poco a poco

Piano Concerto No. 5

("Emperor")
First Movement Excerpt

Ludwig van Beethoven
1770-1827
Op. 73
originally for piano and orchestra

Allegro

original key: E-flat Major

Symphony No. 3

("Eroica")
First Movement Excerpt

Ludwig van Beethoven
1770–1827
Op. 55
originally for orchestra

Allegro con brio

original key: E-flat Major

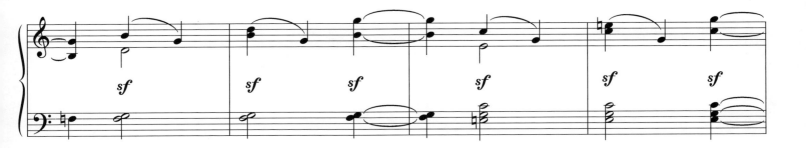

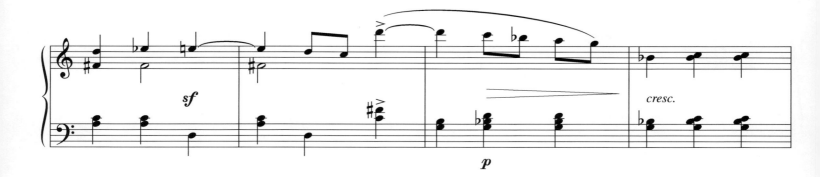

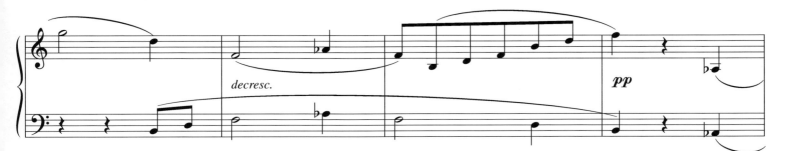

Symphony No. 5
First Movement Excerpt

Ludwig van Beethoven
1770–1827
Op. 67
originally for orchestra

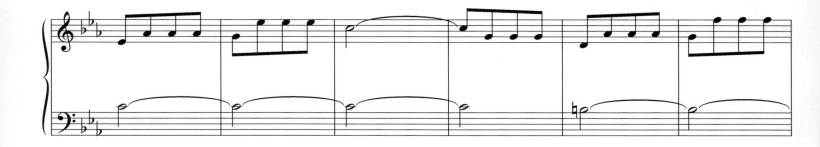

Symphony No. 6 in F Major
("Pastoral")
First Movement Excerpt ("Awakening of cheerful feelings on arrival in the country")

Ludwig van Beethoven
1770-1827
Op. 68
originally for orchestra

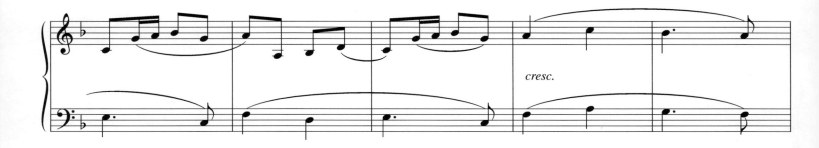

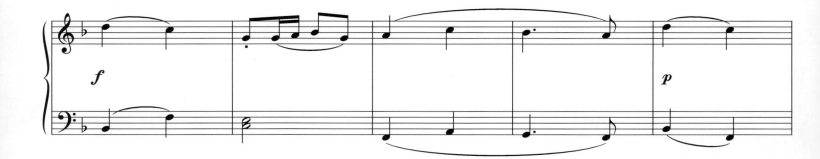

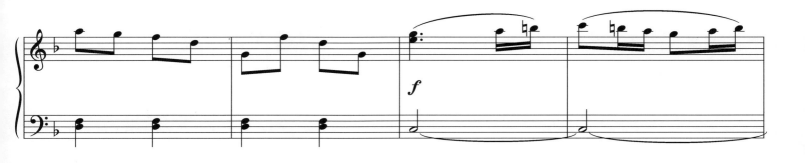

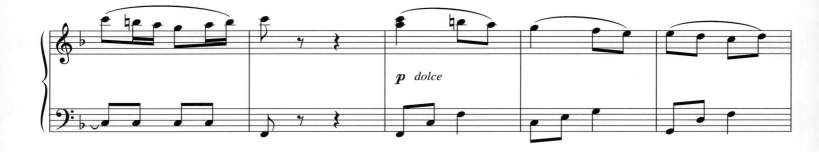

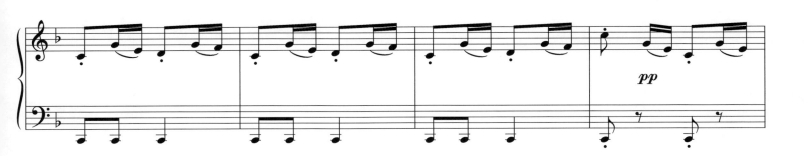

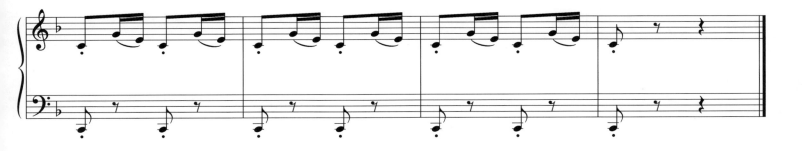

Turkish March

from THE RUINS OF ATHENS

Ludwig van Beethoven
1770-1827
Op. 113
originally for orchestra

160

Che farò senza Euridice
from the opera ORFEO ED EURIDICE

Christoph von Gluck
1714-1787
originally for alto voice and orchestra

Allegretto

163

Tempo I

Moderato

Adagio

Tempo I

Gavotte

François-Joseph Gossec
1734-1829
originally for flute and string quartet

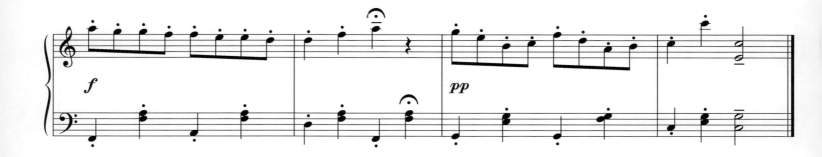

Gypsy Rondo
from Keyboard Trio No. 23 in G Major
Third Movement

Franz Joseph Haydn
1732-1809
originally for violin, violoncello, keyboard

The Heavens Are Telling
from the oratorio THE CREATION

Franz Joseph Haydn
1732-1809
originally for chorus and orchestra

Allegro (♩ = 116)

173

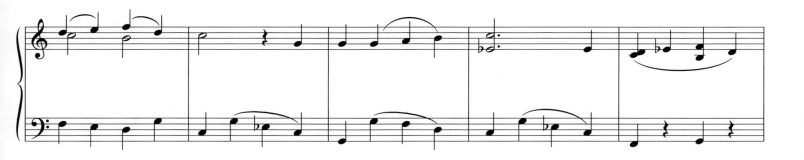

Symphony No. 94
("Surprise")
Second Movement Excerpt

Franz Joseph Haydn
1732-1809
originally for orchestra

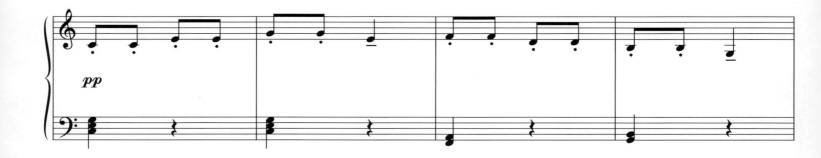

Symphony No. 101
("The Clock")
Third Movement Excerpt

Franz Joseph Haydn
1732-1809
originally for orchestra

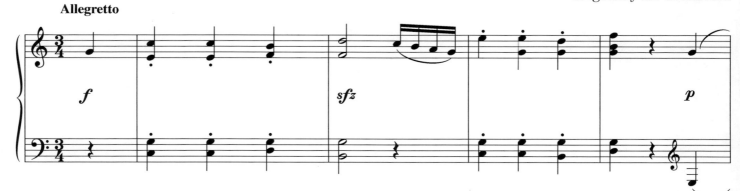

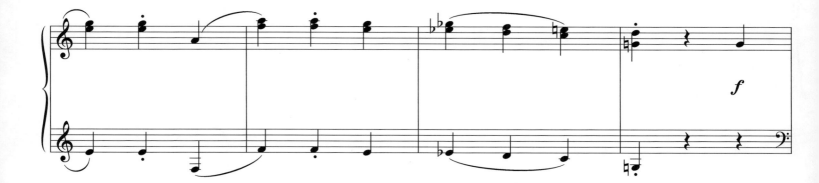

original key: D Major

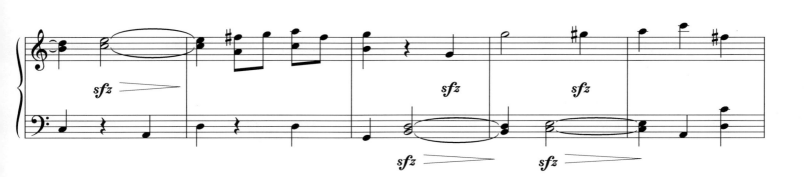

Symphony No. 104
("London")
First Movement Excerpt

Franz Joseph Haydn
1732-1809
originally for orchestra

Allegro

original key: D Major

Alleluia

from the solo motet EXSULTATE, JUBILATE
Excerpt

Wolfgang Amadeus Mozart
1756-1791
K. 165
originally for soprano and orchestra

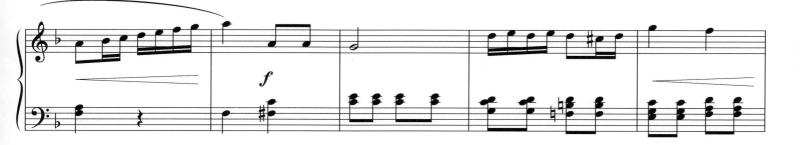

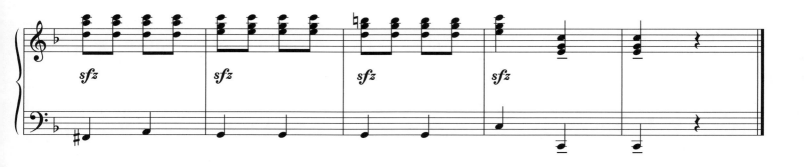

Contessa, perdono

from the opera LE NOZZE DI FIGARO
(The Marriage of Figaro)

Wolfgang Amadeus Mozart
1756–1791
originally for solo voices and orchestra

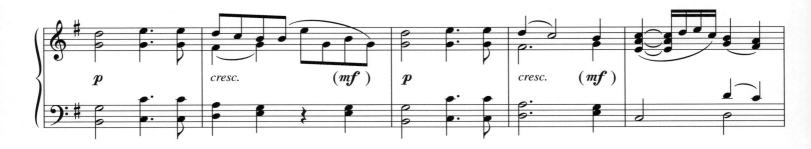

Eine kleine Nachtmusik

(A Little Night Music)
First Movement Excerpt

Wolfgang Amadeus Mozart
1756-1791
K. 525
originally for string ensemble

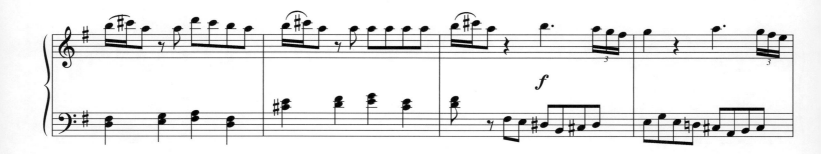

Lacrymosa
from REQUIEM IN D MINOR

Wolfgang Amadeus Mozart
1756-1791
K. 626
originally for chorus and orchestra

Larghetto

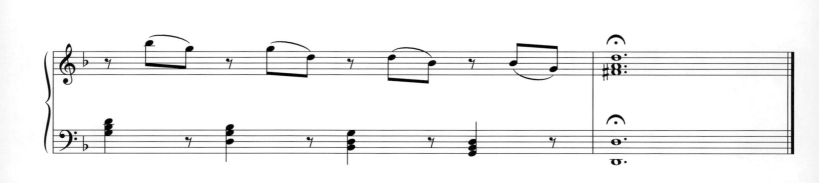

Serenade No. 10 for Winds
Third Movement

Wolfgang Amadeus Mozart
1756–1791
K. 361
originally for woodwinds

original key: E-flat Major

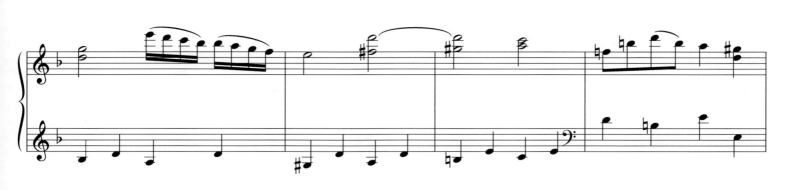

Piano Concerto No. 21
("Elvira Madigan")
Second Movement Excerpt

Wolfgang Amadeus Mozart
1756-1791
K. 467
originally for piano and orchestra

Andante

Symphony No. 29

First Movement Excerpt

Wolfgang Amadeus Mozart
1756-1791
K. 201
originally for orchestra

Allegro moderato

original key: A Major

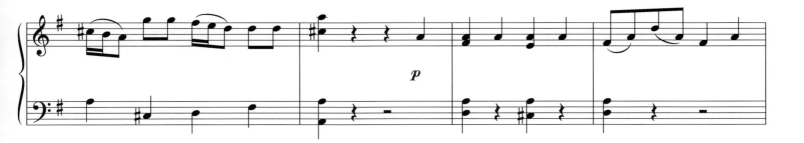

Symphony No. 36
("Linz")
First Movement Excerpt

Wolfgang Amadeus Mozart
1756–1791
K. 425
originally for orchestra

Symphony No. 40

First Movement Excerpt

Wolfgang Amadeus Mozart
1756-1791
K. 550
originally for orchestra

Allegro molto

original key: G Minor

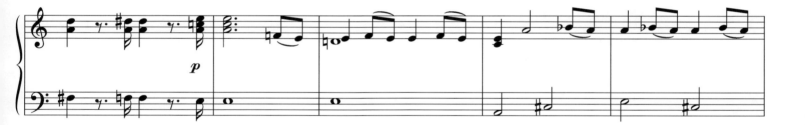

Symphony No. 41

("Jupiter")
First Movement Excerpt

Wolfgang Amadeus Mozart
1756-1791
K. 551
originally for orchestra

Allegro vivace

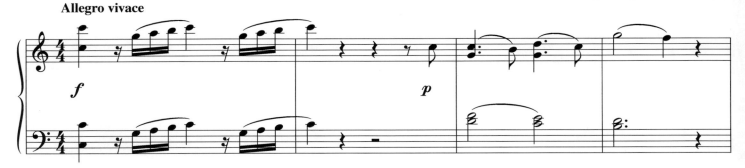

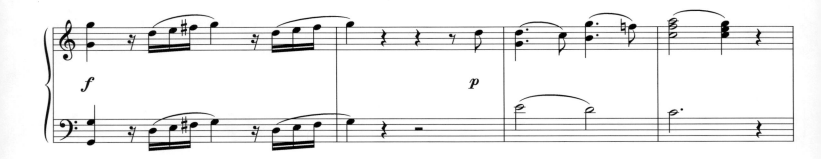

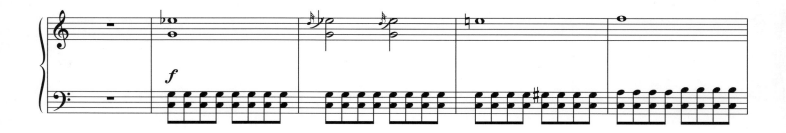